禪修筆記系列 02　Meditation Notes Series, Number 02

One-minute Meditation

Take a deep breath; put your palms together; relax;
quiet down; let your heart return to its origin

By Dharma Master Hsin Tao

「深呼吸，合掌，放鬆，寧靜下來，讓心回到原點。」

釋心道　著

目錄

Table of Contents

The relationship between
one-minute and nine-minute meditation· · 67

編者的話

靈鷲山開山和尚 心道師父自西元二〇〇九年推出一分禪，此可謂平安禪法的一大方便法門。然而，大眾若要透過此方便法門而獲得最大利益，必須要能好好領會一分禪的要訣、精神和意義。

為了這一理由，編者特別從心道師父這兩、三年的相關開示中，選出一分禪的原理與實際操作方法中的要訣內容，以供有志禪修者參考。

另外，禪修是一門非常講求實際操作方法的修行方式，一分禪雖然簡單易行，但希望有志修習者還是能夠盡多參加靈鷲山的各項禪修活動，透過共修而領會這當中的殊勝與奧妙。

靈鷲山三乘研究中心

一分禪的緣起和意義

我們知道，現代人因為外在環境的干擾，或者是經濟上的問題，以至於各式各樣的問題造成身心的不安定，讓我們在生活中常覺得很煩，累積種種內心的問題，造成憂鬱症、躁鬱症，甚至自殺。大環境方面，今天這個地球暖化，到處瀰漫著不寧靜，讓這個地球災難重重。所以，我們一直在推動心和平以至於世界和平的工作。

　　例如，從二〇〇三年起我們每年都舉行萬人禪修活動，在我的親自帶領之下，讓參與民眾體驗平安禪所帶來的和平與寧靜，更希望大家能夠把這種祥和狀態帶進日常生活。到了二〇〇八年，我們推動寧靜、愛心、對話、素食、環保袋、節能、減碳、節水、綠化等愛地球的九大生活主張，把透過禪修而獲得的平安和寧靜擴大為全球寧靜運動，希望藉著具體行動來幫助地球平安，這可說是我常講的「心平安了，世界就平安了」的具體落實方案。

全球所有問題幾乎都是因為我們的「心」出了問題，因此，處理這些問題也是從「心」開始，從內心和平到世界和平，從內心寧靜到整個世界、全球的寧靜。所以，我們推行每天禪坐三次，每次九分鐘的平安禪，以禪修激發內在的能量和直覺，使得身心靈都能夠安靜、寧靜與祥和，並且把這份和平的喜悅影響社會，為世界帶來祥和。

在推行全球寧靜運動時，我們推廣「寧靜手環」，目的無非也在提醒大家，每天抽出時間讓自己寧靜下來，手環的兩面分別是紅色和白色，當白色面朝外，表示心歸零的寧靜狀態；紅面朝外，代表心情浮動。所以「寧靜手環」其實也是愛心手環，愛惜自己和別人的生命，而寧靜也表示愛地球、愛和平的意思，因為寧靜讓地球能夠從種種傷害裡面慢慢康復，手環的白色朝外，就是說我的心非常寧靜，可以幫助很多需要幫助的眾生，紅色朝

外表示心情、情緒不太好，需要別人來幫助，幫助自己把心寧靜下來。

　　在寧靜一切下，我們希望能真正落實禪修精神，真正做到「心平安，世界就平安」。於是我們向大眾推行禪修的方法，把我自身多年禪修經驗的體會與大家分享。不過，在這個忙碌的現代社會裡，不少人甚至連抽出九分鐘的打坐時間都沒有，所以，我們又在最近兩三年藉著推廣全球寧靜運動

的這一時機，推出「一分禪」，透過一分鐘的這種禪修，把整個內心的各種浮躁不定的東西都能在最快速的時間裡面安定下來，這「一分禪」的程序是：

深呼吸、合掌、放鬆、寧靜下來、讓心回到原點。

這一分鐘的禪法，在我們快要生氣、沒辦法忍耐的時候，能很快地寧靜下來，把心回到它本來的原點。然而，「一分禪」的方法雖然簡單易行，但效果要好的話，了解它的要訣和內涵是十分必要的關鍵，這和所有的禪修方法是一樣的，愈是能夠領會這個一分禪的原理，必然更能體會當中的意義，並能讓自己的生命獲得更大的利益。

一分禪的操作口訣

深呼吸、合掌、放鬆、寧靜下來、讓心回到原點。

心道法師

Dharma Master Hsin Tao

一分禪的基本要訣與方法

引言

　　我們的一分鐘禪，就是平日大家在生活當中，工作忙碌的時候，如果心情不好、心裡很煩，想發脾氣、起衝突的時候，只要做這個最簡單的禪修方法，叫做一分禪，方法是「深呼吸，合掌，放鬆，寧靜下來，讓心回到原點。」這不需要幾分鐘，隨

時都可以做，甚至用不著一分鐘，「心」就可以回到原點，整個身心內外都寧靜下來。

　　或許有人會產生疑問，這短短一分鐘，甚至是一分鐘都不到的禪法，真的能有具體的禪修效果嗎？其實，禪修有很多的方法，而這個一分鐘的禪法，它的原理和方法跟我們一直推廣的九分鐘平安禪基本上是相通的。四階動作的九分禪，具體方法分為調身、調呼吸、調心、聽寂靜等內容，簡單來

說，是身與心兩方面的調整、練習，而一分禪的
「深呼吸，合掌，放鬆，寧靜下來，讓心回到原
點」這幾個簡單動作，也是包含了身和心的調和。

深呼吸

我們看這個「一分禪」的口訣只有短短的五句話：「深呼吸，合掌，放鬆，寧靜下來，讓心回到原點。」首先是深呼吸，也就是吐氣和納氣，深呼吸能把我們身體裡面二氧化碳以及很多的這些穢氣吐出來，吸入含氧的空氣，讓我們身體充氧，這第一步口訣的深呼吸動作，不單幫助我們充氧，也使得身心同時能初步的安定下來。

合掌

　　口訣的第二句是「合掌」，合掌的當下即能幫助身心進入安頓的狀態，因為日常生活裡面，我們的心非常雜亂，難以專心，因此，禪修必然講求如何攝心的問題，「一分禪」與其他禪法的主要差異是沒有太多的時間來調心、攝心，但我們這裡有一個幫助大家快速攝心的方法，就是「合掌」。

「合掌」這個動作非常簡單，但其所代表的含義卻十分豐富，「合掌」也稱作「合十」，這個動作可以經常在各種不同宗教儀式中看見，它代表人們向上天或者是諸神的祈禱，也表示尊敬萬物，是人類表達安祥、謙卑的一種十分自然的肢體語言。

　　天台宗的智者大師在《觀音義疏》裡面說：「合掌為敬，手本二邊，今合為一，表不敢散誕，

專至一心；一心相當，故以此表敬也。」所以，在佛法裡面，「合掌」表示專至一心，表達心中的敬意，把散亂的心調好。

因此，在紛擾的日常生活中，「合掌」能夠幫助我們收拾這顆紛亂不安的心，讓心回歸到清淨與安定，並且表示對其他一切眾生的善意釋放，代表了相互的接納與和諧。「合掌」這一簡單的動作，就是把自己心中的和平帶給其他眾生，讓自己和他

人在當下便能夠和平與寧靜。所以，在「一分禪」口訣裡面，這簡單的「合掌」動作，意義非常深遠，而在禪修方面的關鍵意義是幫助我們當下調攝自己的心。

放鬆

　　第三句口訣是「放鬆」,「放鬆」一方面是指
身體的放鬆,我們的身體是由地、水、火、風等四
大元素組合而成,在禪修的時候,身體放鬆是基本
要訣之一,因為唯有放鬆,身體血氣才能暢通,禪
修時才容易入靜。另方面,身與心是息息相關的,
身體是在空間中由地、水、火、風四大組合成,加
上心識而構成完整的有情生命,所以佛法講地、

水、火、風、空、識的六大調和，因此，身體的放鬆必須與心識、心念相互配合，身體若要真的能夠放鬆，心念要能夠放下，放鬆、放下是一體的，能夠放鬆、放下，身與心就可以形成很好的良性循環，這即是禪修時的調身和調心，操作「一分禪」時也一樣，必須放鬆、放下。

寧靜下來

第四句口訣是「寧靜下來」，在這個現代社會裡，我們身心內外都很容易被各式各樣的吵雜資訊所佔據，導致身體僵硬、心念散亂，自己在想什麼也搞不清楚，糊里糊塗就沒有辦法操控自己的想法和做法，可以說整個人被這個爆炸的資訊所控制。因此，第四句口訣是「寧靜下來」，寧靜下來，整個身心內外的能量才可以出來。所以，我們在修平

安禪時，最終的重點是在聆聽安靜、寂靜，這裡修一分禪的時候，沒有太多時間來聆聽寂靜，而是當下要身心寧靜下來，在寧靜當中讓身心祥和，當下契入生命當中的寧靜和平。

讓心回到原點

　　最後的口訣是「讓心回到原點」，禪修多年的經驗告訴我，寧靜、寂靜是我們生命最原始、最源頭的狀態。禪修可以幫助我們回到這一本來面目，因為每個人都具足真理的元素，這是最原始自己的本地風光。

　　平常生活中的自己都是往外馳騁，眼睛看的、耳朵聽的，一切都不是真正的自己，這一感受外在

世界的身體也是處於無常世間當中，一切的有為造作早晚也會是煙消雲散。因此，禪修是為了體驗何謂真正自己的本來，這個表面的自己、自我其實什麼都不是，這個身體就像是每一期生命的衣服一樣，會不斷地被替換，只有原本真實的本來面目不會變。

透過各種禪修方法，找到我們真實、古老的這個存在，就在我們生命當下的這份內在找到永恆，活的時候就可以找得到，天堂就在生命的當下。這

是我多年來在塚間、墳墓等地方修行時的體會，最終必須回到靈性，要一直不斷地回到心的原點。

一般人若是沒有修行的話，生命是呈現為放射式的往外擴散，一直往外放射、消耗生命能量。在做任何禪修功夫的時候，就是要回到我們的靈性、心性，在寧靜、寂靜當中，生命的原點便會顯現，當生命回到原點，便可以看到真正的自己。因為唯有我們的心回到原點，生命才能得到真正的安

頓，而且只有當我們的心真正平安，用這份力量和能量來影響、迴向給其他眾生，世界也才會平安。所以，「一分禪」最後一句的口訣是「讓心回到原點」，回到本自具足的本來面目。

一分禪口訣的總收攝

「深呼吸，合掌，放鬆，寧靜下來，讓心回到原點。」以上我們分析這「一分禪」口訣要領和意義的時候，可以看到口訣的每一個項目內容都有其豐富和深刻的意義，但這種種的深意並不是要大家用意識來分別其內容，而是在理解當下即以真心來體會這要訣的神髓和意義，這份體會愈是深刻真切，修「一分禪」時的效果就愈能彰顯出來。

另外，實際修持「一分禪」的時候，這五項要訣是互為因果的收攝為一體的，是一氣呵成的，從深呼吸、合掌、放鬆、寧靜下來，直至心回到原點，換句話說，這「一分禪」的修持是從身和心的調和當下，即入於寧靜、寂靜的靈性境界。

一分禪與九分禪的關係

　　現在世界各地都有各種不同的小乘、大乘、密乘的禪法傳承，當然，每種禪法的目的都是為了能讓眾生離苦得樂。而靈鷲山主要推廣的是九分鐘的平安禪，這是我自身多年來禪修經驗的體會所歸納出來的方法，從身心的六大調和到最終的靈性快樂，透過這個平安禪的修行，是絕對可以達到的境界。至於這本小冊子談到的「一分禪」，表面上看

似簡單，但其內涵意義是同樣豐富的，也許有人會
疑惑，究竟一分禪與九分禪有什麼關係？修一分禪
是否可代替九分禪？

　　若各位有仔細領會這本「一分禪」小冊子的內
容，必然會發覺一分禪與九分禪的原理是相通的。
簡單的說，對沒有時間修行九分禪的大眾來說，一
分禪是一種方便，由於一分禪原理與九分禪相通，
我們在進行「深呼吸，合掌，放鬆，寧靜下來，讓

心回到原點」這一分禪的內容時，其實已經在心田種下禪悟的清淨種子，因緣成熟時，會更進一步投入修行，自然抽出更多時間來禪修。而對於平日已有修習九分禪的修行者，一分禪是讓他可以隨時隨地都能夠「複習」禪境界的一大方便。

One-minute Meditation

Take a deep breath; put your palms together; relax;
quiet down; let your heart return to its origin

By Dharma Master Hsin Tao

Editor's foreword

In 2009 Master Hsin Tao, the founder of Ling Jiou Mountain, began teaching a type of tranquility practice he refers to as "one-minute meditation." While the emphasis is on simplicity and convenience, in order to gain the greatest benefit from this practice it is necessary to first have a clear understanding of how it's done and what it's all about.

Thus it was decided to extract from Master Hsin Tao's discourses over the past few years passages describing both the theory and practice of one-minute meditation and compile them into a booklet for the convenience of those who would like to learn this practice.

Despite the emphasis on simplicity, meditation can be a very challenging practice. Thus, in addition to this written introduction, it is best to also have personal guidance by attending a meditation class at Ling Jiou Mountain.

Triyāna Research Center, Ling Jiou Mountain

The origin and meaning of one-minute meditation

Due to a wide variety of reasons—from financial difficulties to natural catastrophes—people living in modern society experience high levels of stress, giving rise to all sorts of mental and physical ailments; some even see suicide as the only solution to their problems. This is why we are putting so much effort into promoting both inner peace and world peace.

One example is the "Meditation for All" activity which we have been holding since 2003.

Participants are provided with personal guidance in tranquility meditation, and the emphasis is on experiencing inner peace and then integrating it into one's daily life.

In 2008 we implemented an environmental awareness campaign called "Nine Ways for Loving the Earth," as well as the "Inner Peace Movement," a way of making the tranquility of meditation the starting point of world peace.

All of these activities are a way of giving concrete expression to what I mean by my motto, "When the mind is peaceful, then the world is peaceful."

Actually, most of the problems in the world stem from the *heart* and *mind* (which is the same word in Chinese). That's why it is so important to start with the mind; that's why world peace begins with inner peace.

I encourage everybody to practice "nine-minute meditation" three times every day as a way of relaxing the body and mind, and awakening one's intuition and innate capabilities; then you can share your own peace and happiness with all of society, with the whole world.

In conjunction with the Inner Peace Movement we came up with the "tranquility bracelet," which is simply a way of reminding ourselves to cultivate a peaceful mind throughout the day. One side of the bracelet is red and the other is white.

When we have the white side facing out, this means that we are in a tranquil state of mind; if, however, we are feeling disturbed or agitated, we flip it over so that the red side is facing out. So this can actually be regarded as a "love bracelet," since it's about loving oneself, others, peace, and the whole world.

In fact, this kind of love and tranquility is an essential part of protecting and healing the Earth. When the white side is facing out, this means that we are feeling calm and centered, and therefore able to benefit others. But if the red side is facing out, this means that we are agitated or disturbed, and need someone to help us calm down and regain our composure.

This is what is meant by "meditation in action," what I mean when I say, "When the heart is at peace, then the world is at peace." This is the reason I teach meditation and share with others what I've learned over many years of practice.

Yet, people today are so busy that many find it difficult to find even nine minutes for meditation. This is why over the past few years we have made "one-minute meditation" a key element of the Inner Peace Movement, for this is a very quick way to settle an agitated mind and regain a sense of peace and clarity.

One-minute meditation consists of five steps: taking a deep breath; joining the palms together in front of the chest; relaxing; quieting down and letting the heart return to its origin.

When we are getting angry or impatient, we can use this technique to quickly calm down and regain a sense of inner composure.

Although one-minute meditation is basically a simple practice, as with all meditation techniques, it is necessary to first have a firm grasp of the key principles involved; i.e., the better we understand how to practice and how it works, the better the results.

Formula for practicing one-minute meditation

Take a deep breath; put your palms together; relax; quiet down; let your heart return to its origin

How to practice

Introduction

Once you learn how to use the one-minute meditation technique, if in the midst of your daily activities you begin to feel stressed out, perturbed, or agitated, all you have to do is remember these five steps: Take a deep breath; put your palms together; relax; quiet down; let your heart return to its origin.

The beauty of this technique is that it doesn't require much time, for by using it the mind quickly returns to a state of equilibrium and you regain your inner and outer composure.

Some may doubt that you can get any real results in less than one minute. Actually, of the many different ways to practice meditation, one-minute meditation is quite similar to the nine-minute meditation technique that we often teach, which consists of four steps: calming the body; calming the breath, calming the mind, and listening to the sound of silence.

To put it simply, both of these techniques are ways of harmonizing the body and mind.

Taking a deep breath

One-minute meditation consists of five simple steps: Take a deep breath; put your palms together; relax; quiet down; and let your heart return to its origin.

We start with taking a deep breath because this is a way of expelling the stale air from the lungs and replacing it with fresh, oxygenated air. In addition to invigorating the body by increasing our oxygen intake, taking a deep breath also calms the body and mind.

Putting the palms together

Joining the palms together in front of the chest *(añjali)* is a way of settling both body and mind. In the midst of our daily lives, the mind tends to be very fickle and scattered. This is why Ch`an meditation give so much emphasis on focusing the mind.

The distinguishing feature of one-minute meditation is that it is designed to quickly calm the mind in everyday situations; this is where putting the palms together comes in. Although *añjali* is very simple, it is a highly symbolic gesture used in the rituals of many different religions. It is a way of praying to Heaven or God, and also for expressing respect, goodwill, and humility.

In the *Guanyin Yishu* the Tiantai Master Zhizhe writes, "*Añjali* is a way of expressing respect. Bringing the palms together in front of the chest helps to focus the scattered mind. If the mind is focused, it becomes respectful" So in Buddhism, *añjali* signifies concentration and respect, and we can use it in the midst of daily life to reign in and calm down a distracted or agitated mind, and also to express harmony and goodwill towards all sentient beings.

With this simple gesture we can share with others the peace within our hearts and imbue the present moment with a sense of harmony. This is why *añjali* is a key element of one-minute meditation; in addition to its profound symbolic meaning, it also helps us to quickly attain a state of concentration of heart and mind.

Relaxing

We begin by relaxing the body. On the one hand, physical relaxation is a prerequisite of meditation practice, because the body needs to be relaxed for its vital energy to flow freely, facilitating tranquility and concentration. On the other hand, the body and mind are closely interconnected.

In Buddhism, the body is described as consisting of the elements earth, water, fire, wind, and space. Add consciousness to these elements and you have a sentient being.

Only when these six elements are in harmony with each other is it possible to relax. Thus, mental and physical relaxation are inseparable; physical relaxation depends on mental relaxation, and vice versa. As with any type of meditation technique, the practice of one-minute meditation is based on relaxing and letting go.

Quieting down

Living in modern society, we are constantly assailed by all sorts of noise and disturbing news, giving rise to physical tension and mental agitation. It can even get to the point that we are so confused and distracted that we don't even know what we are doing or thinking.

This is why in the fourth step we train ourselves to quiet down, for only when we are peaceful in body, heart and mind will our innate capacities manifest and come into full play.

In the practice of tranquility meditation the emphasis is on listening to the sound of silence, but in one-minute meditation there is not enough time for that. Instead, the focus is on experiencing a degree of peace and tranquility in the present moment.

Letting the heart return to its origin

From many years of meditation practice, I have found that peace and silence are our most essential, most original state of being. Meditation helps us to return to this original state, for this is our essential nature, this is our most basic quality.

In the course of daily life we tend to constantly gravitate towards the outer world. But what we see and hear, whatever we encounter through the senses, even the body itself, is impermanent and conditioned, and thus not who we really are.

Meditation is a way of returning to our true origin. Even our personality and ordinary sense of identity are ephemeral and superficial. The body is rather like clothing that we wear for some years before discarding it and replacing it with something else. The only thing that doesn't change is our original, essential nature.

The ultimate goal of all types of meditation techniques is to lead us back to our true, original nature. This is something which exists eternally in the present moment; not something that we experience after death, but something immanent, something that we can find here and now.

This is what I've learned over the course of many years of meditation practice, especially in graveyards. To experience our true spiritual nature, which is the ultimate goal of meditation, we have to constantly let our heart and mind return to their origin.

Without spiritual practice, the tendency is to continually direct our attention outwards, and this is how most of our energy is expended. By contrast, with meditation we are training ourselves to return to our true spiritual nature, to the nature of the heart and mind itself.

Dwelling in a state of tranquility, our true nature manifests all by itself, revealing who and what we really are. Only by returning the mind to its source can we experience genuine peace; and by tapping into this source of profound peace we naturally have a wholesome influence on others and the whole world. This is why in the final step of the one-minute meditation we let our heart and mind return to their origin and discover our original, essential nature – our original face before we were born.

Using one-minute meditation to focus the mind

We need to clearly understand the purpose and importance of each of these five steps, but we also need to avoid the pitfall of overanalyzing it to the point that the practice becomes merely an intellectual exercise.

We need to use intuitive awareness to gain an experiential understanding of the essential meaning of these five steps, and the better we can do this, the better the results.

Also, these five steps function simultaneously as an organic whole in helping to focus the mind and letting the heart return to its origin. In other words, one-minute meditation is a way of experiencing peace and tranquility in the present moment by harmonizing body and mind, by quieting down and entering the realm of the spirit which is completely still and at peace.

The relationship between one-minute and nine-minute meditation

There are many different meditation practices taught in various Buddhist traditions, but they all have the same ultimate goal of leading us to genuine happiness and freedom from stress.

The main meditation practice taught at Ling Jiou Mountain is nine-minute meditation, a practice which I formulated based on my meditation experience over the course of many years. It's a practical and effective practice which starts with awareness of the six elements and culminates in spiritual joy. While one-minute meditation may seem to be excessively simple, it does bring profound results.

However, some may be wondering about the difference between the two, and if it's sufficient to only practice one-minute meditation.

As can be seen by carefully reading this booklet, one-minute meditation and nine-minute meditation are based on the same principles. To put it simply, one-minute meditation is a skilful means for those who don't have enough time to practice nine-minute meditation.

Since they are both based on the same principles, you might say that practicing one-minute meditation is a way of sowing the seeds of awakening; later on, when we encounter the appropriate causes and conditions, these seeds will sprout, making it much easier to spend more time and energy on meditation.

In addition, for those who already practice nine-minute meditation regularly, one-minute meditation is a skilful means which can be used at any time and place to tap into the wisdom and serenity they have already cultivated in their regular practice.

多羅觀音

慈視大海的多羅觀音，憶護眾生，濟度一切有情。

Duoluo Guanyin

Overlooking the Pacific Ocean like a loving mother, Guanyin (Avalokiteśvara) watches over and delivers all beings from suffering.

One-minute meditation

One-minute meditation

Duoluo Guanyin

One-minute meditation

天眼門

空中的天眼，透視虛空，象徵澈見諸法空性。柱石則刻有各宗教圖騰，體

Gate of the Divine Eye

Tianyan (divine eye) refers to the vision of emptiness in which all things are clearly discerned. It also symbolizes the full realization of Dharma. Supported by two stone totem poles carved with ancient symbols from various religions, it shows the ideals of "Respect, Tolerance, and Love."

One-minute meditation

One-minute meditation

One-minute meditation

法輪雙鹿

閃耀金色光芒的法輪雙鹿，代表佛陀的法教，象徵法輪常轉，普傳十方。

Falun (Dharma Wheel) Twin Deer

Brilliantly shining in golden light, the Falun Twin Deer stand for the Buddha's teachings, and also show the ceaseless turning of the Dharma Wheel in all places.

One-minute meditation

One-minute meditation

One-minute meditation

五百羅漢步道

環山步道上錯落安奉的羅漢像，彷若演述著
佛陀時代的聖眾弟子行誼。

Arhat Path

Scattered along the main path circling the Ling Jiou Mountain are the stone images of the 500 Arhats, commemorating the attainments of the Buddha's disciples.

One-minute meditation

One-minute meditation

One-minute meditation

鷲首石

開山聖殿與祖師殿岩間,突出一塊巨石,狀如鷲首,
巧映古印度靈鷲山上的鷲首石。

Vulture's Head Rock

Among the rocks between the Founders Hall and the Patriarchs Hall, a huge boulder in the shape of a vulture's head rises up out of the earth. And it bears a striking resemblance to the boulder on the top of Vulture's Peak in ancient India.

One-minute meditation

One-minute meditation

One-minute meditation

Vulture's Head Rock

佛足

普賢道場上，以巨石雕刻的佛足，象徵著實踐以及行願的普賢精神。

Footprint of the Buddha

On the Samantabhadra Terrace there is a "footprint of the Buddha" carved into a large boulder, symbolizing Samantabhadra's spirit of practicing and putting vows into action.

One-minute meditation

One-minute meditation

One-minute meditation

Footprint of the Buddha

塔林

造型殊異、特色各具的佛塔，
呈現了靈鷲山三乘合一的特色，
形成殊勝的塔林景觀。

Stupa Area

With different shapes and styles, the stupas in the Stupa Area show the Ling Jiou Mountain's characteristic of "the three vehicles as one" and form a sacred landscape.

One-minute meditation

One-minute meditation

One-minute meditation

十一面觀音

十一面觀音象徵觀音菩薩度化眾生的巧善化現，
當以何身得度者，便現何相而度之。

Eleven-Faced Guanyin

This Eleven-faced Guanyin is one the Bodhisattva Guanyin's forms to watch over all sentient beings and deliver them from suffering. The Bodhisattva takes on different forms to skillfully free all beings from rebirth.

One-minute meditation

One-minute meditation

Eleven-Faced Guanyin

One-minute meditation

Eleven-Faced Guanyin

《禪修筆記系列 02》

一分禪

作　　者：釋心道
總 策 劃：釋了意

編　　審：靈鷲山研究暨出版中心
主　　編：洪淑妍
責任編輯：阮馨儀
美術編輯：宋明展

發 行 人：歐陽慕親
出版發行：財團法人靈鷲山般若文教基金會附設出版社
地　　址：23444新北市永和區保生路2號21樓
電　　話：(02)2232-1008
傳　　真：(02)2232-1010
網　　址：www.093books.com.tw
讀者信箱：books@ljm.org.tw

法律顧問：永然聯合法律事務所
印　　刷：國宣印刷有限公司
初版一刷：2012年4月
定　　價：250元
I S B N：978-986-6324-20-8

《Meditation Notes Series, Number 02》

One-minute Meditation

Author：Dharma Master Hsin Tao
Overall design：Bhikkhuni Liaoyi

Producer：Ling Jiou Mountain Research and Publication Center
Chief editor：Shuyen Hung
Executive editor：Hsinyi Juan
Art editor：Mingzhan Song
English translation：Ken Kraynak、Maria Reis Habito

Publisher：Ouyang, Mu-qin
Distributer：Prajñā Cultural Foundation of Ling Jiou Mountain
Address：No. 2, Floor 21, Baosheng Road, Yonghe District, New Taipei City, 23444

Telephone：(02)2232-1008
Fax：(02)2232-1010
Website ：www.093books.com.tw
Comments：books@ljm.org.tw

Legal consultant：Perennial Group Law Firm
Printer：Golden Sun Printing
First edition：2012/4
List price：NT$250
I S B N：978-986-6324-20-8

國家圖書館出版品預行編目（CIP）資料

一分禪 / 釋心道著 -- 初版 -- 新北市：靈鷲山
般若出版，2012.04
面；公分 --（禪修筆記系列；2）
ISBN 978-986-6324-20-8
1.佛教修持 2.佛教說法
225.87　　　　　　　　　　101006606